KT-481-314

CONTENTS

CHAPTER ONE
YOU ROCK AND RULE
– no really, you do!

QUIZ: WHAT ARE YOU LIKE?

What to do…Read the following statements and
tick any you agree with:

Most of the time I'm really happy
Agree ☐   Disagree ☐

I find it hard to make new friends
Agree ☐   **Disagree** ☐

I'm the loudest of all my friends
Agree ☐   Disagree ☐

Get to
know the
real you!

7 776207 14

THE **mizz** ®

GUIDE TO LIFE!

North Lanarkshire Council Motherwell Library Hamilton Road, Motherwell **NEH**	
7 776207 14	
Askews	27-Nov-2009
J646.7	£4.99
	322491

Text copyright © Panini UK Ltd 2009
Illustrations: Joanna Baldock. Copyright © Panini UK Ltd 2009
Cover photography: Shutterstock

With special thanks to:
Joanna Baldock, Lisa Clark, Kate Miller,
Karen O'Brien and Alan O'Keefe.

Published in Great Britain in 2009
by Panini Books

All rights reserved. Apart from any use permitted under UK copyright law,
this publication may only be reproduced, stored or transmitted, in any form,
or by any means with prior permission in writing of the publishers or in the
case of reprographic production in accordance with the terms of licences
issued by the Copyright Licensing Agency.

A catalogue record of this book is available from the British Library.

ISBN: 978-1-84653-106-4

Printed and bound in England by Clays Ltd, St Ives plc

Panini Books a division of Panini UK Ltd.
Brockbourne House, 77 Mount Ephraim, Tunbridge Wells, Kent, TN4 8BS

Virgin Pulp used during manufacture of the paper has been sourced
from sustainably managed forests certified by the Pan European Forest
Certification (PEFC) organisation.

I find it hard to discuss my problems
Agree ❑   **Disagree** ❑

I'd never dare to ask a guy out
Agree ❑   **Disagree** ❑

I really love meeting new people
Agree ❑   Disagree ❑

I often worry about saying the wrong thing
Agree ❑   **Disagree** ❑

My friends come to me for advice
Agree ❑   Disagree ❑

I don't need a boyfriend to feel happy
Agree ❑   Disagree ❑

I get tongue-tied when I talk to lads
Agree ❑   **Disagree** ❑

My parents don't understand me
Agree ❑   **Disagree** ❑

Sometimes I feel really un-cool
Agree ❑   **Disagree** ❑

I don't care if people like me or not
Agree ❑   Disagree ❑

I'm always the first to answer questions in class
Agree ❑   Disagree ❑

I'm always coming up with ideas for days out with my mates
Agree ❑   Disagree ❑

Score three for every bold answer you ticked, and one for every plain. Then read on for your self-savvy score…

If you scored 14 – 22
You're a shy sister
You don't like drawing attention to yourself and worry about speaking out. And there's nothing wrong with that unless it stops you doing the things that you want to. Try this trick: write a list of your achievements and look back at it whenever you need a boost.

If you scored 23 – 32
You're a cool customer
Mostly you're pretty confident, but there are times when you're uncertain – like when you're facing a new situation. If you feel down, try talking to your mates. You'll probably find they feel the same way, and they'll give you the support you need.

If you scored 33 – 42
You're a feisty female
You're one of those lucky girls who naturally feels happy with herself. You're outgoing and confident, and love meeting new people because you're hardly ever shy with strangers. Go girl!

BECOME A KICK-BUTT QUEEN!

GO FROM INVISIBLE TO INVINCIBLE...

If the guy you're crushing on doesn't know you exist or you constantly compare yourself to pouty-faced model types, chances are your self-esteem is taking a serious bashing. You rock, so instead of fretting about the size of your butt, shake it on the dance floor, because it's time to boost your bravado!

BODY TALK

Your body can speak as loud as the words you say, so show people you've got it going on without saying a word!

`WALK TALL` Pull those shoulders back and walk like you're proud of who you are, soon enough you'll actually 100% believe it.

`MAKE EYE CONTACT` There's no more obvious low-confidence giveaway than someone who can't make eye contact, so drag your gaze off the floor and look people directly in their eyes, it's a great way to express interest – both in other people or in your surroundings.

`UNFOLD YOUR ARMS` If they're locked across your chest, you're sending out a clear message that you're a no-go area. Use them instead to make you seem super enthusiastic – wide hand gestures imply openness and small hand gestures can emphasise what you're saying. Take care not to over-use them though, you don't want to scare people away!

`SMILE` Even when you least feel like it. Not only does a smile make you to look so much more approachable, it's the perfect accessory guaranteed to set off any fashion ensemble!

DEAL WITH IT!

If you're not feeling confident yet, tackle your confidence breakers with these fail-safe techniques and ooze self-esteem and charm whatever the situation…

Confidence breaker: "I don't like the way I look"

What is it you really don't like? Is it your eye colour? A spot break out? The way your hair won't ever do what it should? Well, there's some stuff you can change – for instance, if your hair's getting you down, go to a good salon for a consultation. The stylist will be able to advise you on how to keep your hair looking fab. If it's something more permanent, like your freckles or your height, then it's all about loving what you've got. Comparing yourself to others is a fast track to Doomsville. Accept yourself for who you are, even your worse bits and learn to love what's great about you!

Confidence breaker: "I'm not clever"

Don't believe you! Okay, so you might struggle with fractions or hate spending time in the art room, but you're probably a star on the hockey pitch or kick-ass at writing essays. The key to surviving school – and having a brilliant career at the end of it all – is finding your top skills and working on that. So if you love writing, get a short story published in the school magazine. Or if French is your thing, find out if there's a foreign exchange you can go on. Building up your self-esteem in the classroom will get you noticed for all the right reasons – go girl!

Confidence breaker: "I'll never get a boyfriend"

Hold it! Are you one of those girls who think their lives would be perfect if only they had a guy on their arm? Forget it! While boys are nice to look at, a sure-fire way to feel super confident is to hang out with your girl gang doing the things you love to do. When you're good to yourself, your confidence will soar and you will turn the heads of cute guys on a regular basis. Just be sure to find a guy who shares your sense of humour and is into the same things as you, that way you know you're onto a winner!

SHORT CUTS TO CONFIDENCE

Make yourself feel fab all day long by:

BEING NICE TO YOU
Being mates with yourself is the first step to feeling confident. You'll be hanging out with yourself forever, so you'd better kiss and make up!

THINK GOOD THOUGHTS
When you're feeling a little bit nervy, force your mind back to a situation when you felt great – like when you laughed with your friends 'til it hurt. Remember good times for an instant confidence boost.

FACE YOUR FEAR
Whether that's a person, or a task you've been dreading. Even if you're cringing inside, get it over with right now and you'll feel super-confident.

CONTROL YOUR DESTINY
You, and only you can get new things going on in your life, so haul yourself off the sofa and make it happen. Putting something off will only stress you out and slow down your confidence trip.

TRICKY TALK

Do you find it difficult to make small talk with your dream dude? Maybe you want to tell a mate she's upset you, but just don't know how?

Deal with these tricky talk situations by following our top-talking master class and make sure you're never left tongue-tied!

There are some conversations that are just not easy, nerves can take over and turn you into a real sweaty Betty. Dumping a boy. Stressy. Bagging a job. Even worse. Unfortunately, life is always going to throw difficult conversations your way, it's how you handle them that really counts. With a few simple, easy-to-remember techniques, you'll find yourself able to talk to anyone.

★ THE ESSENTIALS FOR A SUCCESSFUL CHAT

`Location:` Don't have an important chat in front of other people, the chances are you'll get flustered, say the wrong thing and get others involved. It's even worse to call the person away from a group by saying 'I need to talk to you' as everyone will want to know what's going on. Catch the person and make a plan to talk later instead.

`Planning:` Knowing what you want to say is important. Be clear about all the things you'd like to cover and try to stick to them, that way you'll be sure that you've said everything you need to.

`Listen:` Speak in a non-aggressive tone and take deep breaths at the end of sentences. This will keep you calm and give the other person the opportunity to respond, if they do, listen to what they say.

★ CHATTING UP MR. SHY

With this chat there are two openers to definitely avoid. It's way too dramatic to start with 'there's something I want to tell you' as is just walking over and blurting out 'I really fancy you' – it'll make you both blush madly. So how do you chat to a shy guy without the embarrassing silences? Often shy boys want to talk but rely on you to lead the conversation. Ask him his opinion on something, like what he thinks of a new band then follow up with shorter questions to let him know you're interested. He'll soon relax and open up to you.

TRICKY TALK TIP

The trick is to make it all sound very casual. Make a plan with some mates, then say to him 'we're all going to the cinema/bowling alley/park on Saturday, it should be fun, do you fancy coming along?' Keep your body language positive with lots of smiles – he will deffo get the message. If he says 'no' don't take it personally: he might not be free. Instead say: 'oh well, maybe next time.'

★ TALKING TO A GIRL WHO YOU WANT TO BE FRIENDS WITH

She's that really cool girl who everyone wants to hang out with because she's always smiling and having fun, so why is she so scary to approach? Answer: *She's not.* Next time you see her hanging out alone, take a deep breath, muster up a pinch of self-confidence and add lots of smiles. Start with a simple 'Hi' and without being super nosey, ask her questions about herself, like 'where did you get that swim bag? It's adorable!' She will be flattered by your interest and will instantly want to talk with you more. People find it easy to talk about themselves and if they enjoy your company they will become your friend.

TRICKY TALK TIP

Remember, compliments go a long way. Tell her that you're digging her footwear and was wondering where she got them from, not only will the person be super flattered, they'll also know you're a girl with the same impeccable taste who they will want to be friends with!

★ GETTING A JOB

Once you've decided where you might like to work to earn your much-needed cash, make a list of all the reasons you'd be a great asset to your-soon-to-be workplace and with a confident smile on your face ask to speak to the manager. Boss types are busy types so be sure to be clear and concise, let them know you're interested in working for them and the reasons why and leave your contact details with a typed résumé (CV).

TRICKY TALK TIP

Being prepared is essential, this way you send out a super positive message that you're a totally employable go-for it girl! Think of some questions before you get there as this will show that you have really thought about the job and are genuinely interested in working there.

QUESTIONS YOU COULD ASK

Say "Do you mind if I ask you a few questions?"

What are the day-to-day duties of the job?
Will I be given training and development?
Who should I report to?
Will I be able to take on more challenges?

Now think of some questions you could ask for the job that you want.

HOW TO SAY NO!

Ever feel like everyone wants something from you? And even though you want to say no, you say yes. You're afraid you'll hurt their feelings, right?

It's important to be a nice person, but sadly it doesn't always pay to be sweet. Sometimes people take advantage of a lovely nature and walk all over you. Here's how to kick butt when you need to, in the nicest possible way!

BORROW-HAPPY FRIENDS

They beg to borrow those cute-as-a-button new leopard print pumps that you haven't even worn yet – or a fiver. So you let them.

If your friend still hasn't paid you back from the last time you lent her cash, and now she's asking again, or if your stuff keeps getting returned with stains – or not at all and you feel completely taken advantage of, it's time to draw the line. If you don't, you'll end up resenting your friend. Say, "I promised myself I wouldn't give anymore loans until people pay me back." Or if it's an item of clothing or a DVD, say, "I know you'd be careful, but I've decided not to lend it to anyone. I hope you understand." If she's a real friend, she totally should.

AGONY AUNT

You're a good listener and love helping your friends out, but lately you feel like their personal agony aunt.

If mates' problems are getting you down, it's time to be cruel to be kind. It won't make you a bad person, it will just stop you getting crazy mad with them. Don't stay on the phone for hours when you don't feel like it, just say, "I'm sorry but I have to go – can I call you tomorrow to see if you're OK?" Learn to start saying how you feel. Being honest isn't the same as being nasty. Friendship is about give and take and you shouldn't have to do all the giving. Being strong will earn you respect.

THE NOTE-COPIERS

You study hard, get good marks and take the best notes in class. You don't mind helping people out from time to time, but now everyone wants to copy them.

You go to class and pay attention, so why should the girls who text all lesson still get to pass their tests courtesy of you? If it's a friend who's always asking, say, "The first few times you needed to copy, I was cool with it. But maybe I can show you how to take better ones of your own from now on." She'll either agree or realise she's being lazy and stop asking. If it's not a close friend who asks, just politely decline and say you need the notes for later. Don't feel like you need to explain.

GOSSIP GIRLS

Get-togethers with your gal pals are starting to resemble the four-way phone conversation between The Plastics in *Mean Girls*.

When mates pressure you to be mean about a mutual friend who's not there, it can be hard not to join in – even though you know it's wrong. But remind yourself, if they bitch about her, they'll probably bitch about you too, which should make it easier for you to make a stand. The simplest way to protest is to say nothing. That way you'll have a clear conscience without losing face. But if you feel brave enough to say something, just say you'd rather not get involved.

LIL' MISS LET DOWN

Your friend is fun to be with but you can't rely on her for anything. She's always late to meet you, forgets your birthday every year, and you're inseparable until a guy comes along and then you don't see her for dust.

A friend like this is rarely doing it to be mean. Usually, it's because you're allowing her to get away with it. So stop making excuses for her and don't accept a half-hearted apology. Next time she upsets you, don't say. "It's OK," say, "Actually, you've ruined my day/hurt me. It's not good enough and I wouldn't do it to you. Please don't do it again." She won't change overnight and you might need to say it a couple of times before you get results, but if you make it clear your friendship needs to be earned, she should start to make more of an effort.

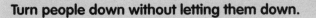

GET TOUGH

Turn people down without letting them down.

Speak up — when you want people to take you seriously, turn up your volume switch and say it like you mean it. This way people will know that no means no and will be less likely to persuade you to say yes.

Be clear - when turning someone down, use 'I' phrases like "I feel…" or "I think…" so they know it's a choice you're making for yourself and not against them.

Don't apologise — never say sorry for being strong and staying true to what you want.

Don't be mean — ultimately always treat other people with the same good grace that you would like to be treated with in return.

Charm School

Want to be the girl everyone wants to sit with at lunchtime? Take a trip to charm school and find out how to work your popularity factor!

Ever wondered why some girls just seem to rock 'n' rule at whatever they do? You know the type, the girl that gets the buff boy, the cool clique of girl mates and gets good marks in Maths? It's because the girl's got charm and she's able to work it like a pair of fabulous heels! The good news? You can get it too!

Charm is not just a cute accessory for your school bag, it's a great way to get dates, mates, parents and teachers eating out of your hand! So it's time to take a class in charm and cast a spell of fabulousness over everyone you meet!

BE PREPARED

Charming people always have something to talk about whatever the situation, so be prepared. You could carry a conversation piece – an interesting piece of jewellery, a cute bag that you've customised yourself, a pin badge with your favourite slogan or catch phrase – anything that will break the ice or prompt people to ask you about it. When they do, have a little story ready, ("Oh this scarf? Well, funny you should ask actually...") Don't, however, prepare and rehearse actual statements or jokes as you'll sound like an extra from a really, really bad daytime soap opera.

SMILE

Smiling is an Access All Areas pass to popularity. Can't think of anything to say? Smile! Not a Miley Cyrus perma-grin but a genuine spill-over smile. Look the person you're talking to in the eyes, then let a slow smile build up on your whole face in the same way you would if Danny Mcfly were to walk in the room – minus the whole jumping up and down and screaming obviously. It'll give you a sincere smile, not a people-pleasing phoney one, making you seem friendly and enthusiastic without saying a single word!

LISTEN UP

Most people love to talk about themselves. And they love it even more when you seem genuinely interested in what they say. Make eye contact, and act like the person you are talking to is the only person in the room. It's a huge compliment to have someone's undivided attention — mates will trust you with secrets and parents and teachers will be completely blown away with your focus. If you find yourself facing someone who you have absolutely nothing in common, instead of yawning out loud, consider it an opportunity to learn about something new. Ask questions and genuinely listen to the answers. It really makes the convo flow better. People will talk about what a wonderful person you are, even if they're not entirely sure why!

BODY TALK

Gesticulate wildly. Okay, not completely wildly as you don't want to poke your soon-to-be friend in the eye, but a little hand motion can go a long way to showing interest and enthusiasm. Also, physical contact can work wonders to increase your bond with someone – girl or guy. Whether it's a simple brush of the hand, or a full-on hug, you'll send them instant 'love me' signals. No mad octopus impressions though, just keep it to a non-threatening zone on their body like the arm.

'ME' CHECK

It's not a competition y'know, so no matter how tempting it might be to respond with "funny, that reminds me of the time I met Orlie Bloom!" make sure you let others enjoy the spotlight. It is really annoying when people always bring the conversation back to themselves, so keep those 'me's' in check. Listening properly involves making the conversation completely distraction free – that means no sneaky texting, okay?

Your Charm School checklist

Don't risk being a Charm School dropout, here's what you need and how to get it...

☑ **CHARISMA** Love who you are. Stand up straight, move around to appear enthusiastic and lean slightly forward when talking to people and you'll instantly send 'I'm a fab person' waves surging through any room!

☑ **MAKE OTHERS FEEL IMPORTANT** Let people know they matter and you enjoy being around them, develop a genuine smile, nod when they talk, briefly touch them on the upper arm, and maintain eye contact.

☑ **GENUINE INTEREST IN OTHERS** Dare to care. Ask after a friend's brother if he's been poorly, ask your teacher how her new puppy is doing, this will show how warm and friendly you are and that you actually remember and care about what's going on in other people's lives.

☑ **GENEROUS** You can be generous in lots of ways – if a friend is moving, offer your time to help her pack, if your bestie hasn't a thing to wear on her first date offer her first pick of your wardrobe. Doing good things for others is a win-win sitch, your friends think you're fab and you'll feel all warm and fuzzy for your good deed.

☑ **BE REAL** Most importantly, be genuine and be yourself. This is when you will feel most relaxed and people will feel good in your company.

Remember, true charm comes from within so find ways to be yourself and share your already rather wonderful personality with everyone around you!

CHAPTER TWO
BODY TALK – BAFFLED BY YOUR BOD?
Not anymore!

LOOKING GOOD!

Do you love what you see when you look in the mirror? Let's find out...

You go shopping with your gal-pals and they're trying on clothes, do you:
A Watch but don't join in as you'd look awful in everything. ☐
B Try everything on too, it'll be fun! ☐

You sleep through your alarm and have to get ready in a rush. Before leaving the house you take a look in the mirror, do you:
A Pull a face at your reflection and search for a paper bag to put over your head. ☐

B Tie your hair back, dab on some lip gloss and blow
yourself a kiss.   ❑

**You're at a party, throwing some serious shapes on the dance floor
when you notice a group of girls looking over, do you:**
A Stop immediately and blush with embarrassment.   ❑
B Smile at them safe in the knowledge that they're loving the
moves you're busting.   ❑

When you get home, you can hardly contain your yawns, do you:
A Lay awake thinking about how great everyone else looked.   ❑
B Clean off your make-up and fall straight to sleep, you're so
tired after all that dancing!   ❑

**You're watching the TV when they introduce a new girl group,
do you:**
A Instantly compare yourself to them and realise they've got
skinnier legs, a smaller tummy and glossier hair than you.   ❑
B Turn your nose up at the music but love the dress the lead
singer is wearing.   ❑

MOSTLY A'S
Too much time spent
comparing yourself to others
and worrying about what
other people think of you
means that life can become
dull and a little depressing!
Try not to compare yourself to
anyone else, you're fab and
unique and that's something
you should celebrate and
shout about!

MOSTLY B'S
You know that nobody is
perfect so instead of getting
hung up on the bits you
don't like, you celebrate and
enhance the good stuff.
There are even times when
you embrace the not-so-
good bits anyway, because
you know that when it all
comes together, it makes an
awesome version of you.

YOUR BODY: SUSSED

Your body is growing in all directions, hair is sprouting here and there and your period is a complete mystery – whether your body changes seem exciting, embarrassing, irritating, or anxiety-producing, don't freak out, we've got everything you need to get sussed about puberty's body makeover.

So, what's actually happening? Puberty is when your body gets an upgrade in preparation for becoming a woman. You develop breasts, your hips become wider and you start your menstrual cycles (periods). During this time, your hormones are all over the place too, which can leave you feeling tearful and anxious at times. Although the changes (or lack of changes) happening to your body may seem scary, it's all completely normal. Puberty can kick in at any time between the ages of eight and sixteen and the good news is that everyone goes through it, just not necessarily at the same time. So don't panic if your friends start developing before you – it's not a race, y'know!

PERIODS – WHAT'S THE DEAL?

Cramps, backache, bloating and mood swings – owwww. Here's the deal...

Getting your period means your body has reached the stage where it's able to have a baby, and once a month it gets revved-up for possible motherhood. When your menstrual cycle starts, your ovaries release an egg that travels through your fallopian tubes into your uterus. If the egg isn't fertilised by a sperm, it will disintegrate along with the womb lining and leave your body. That's your period!

How long will my period last?
Periods tend to last between three and seven days and although

it may seem like you're losing a lot of blood, you're actually not. Your body only loses between 35 to 40ml of blood a month (about two tablespoons worth).

Sanitary towels or tampons – what's best?

You should use whatever you feel comfy with. Most girls start with towels (which line the inside of your knickers) because they're easy to use. Towels come in different absorbancies to suit your flow. But once you start practising with tampons (which are inserted into your vagina) you'll find it easy to get the hang of them too. Tampons can be really handy if you want play sports or wear your fave skinny jeans!

All my friends have started and I haven't, why?

Don't panic. Periods can start any time between the ages of nine and 17. The best way to predict when you'll start is to ask your female relatives when they started, as it can be hereditary.

HOW DO I STAMP OUT PERIOD PAIN?

★ Exercise helps to stabilise your hormone levels – so whether it's a walk around the park or dancing to your favourite tune – get moving to ease the pain.

★ Eat regularly to keep your energy levels up. Wholemeal bread, nuts, fruit, green veg and fish will replace the nutrients (magnesium, iron and zinc, vitamins E and B) your body is losing. Avoid caffeine.

HAVE A WARM BATH TO RELAX THOSE TUMMY CRAMPS!

★ Unwind in a warm bath to relax your cramped muscles and settle on the sofa with a hot water bottle.

HORMONE CHANGES – THE ROLLER COASTER RIDE!

On top of the world in the morning, depressed over lunch time and angry in the evening? Blame your hormones. During puberty, your body starts producing hormones. While these hormones cause physical changes in your body, they also cause emotional changes too.

Why does my mood flip from happy to sad without warning?

Any changes in the level of oestrogen and progesterone hormones, (these are the hormones you produce to keep your reproductive system in check) like having your period, can cause major irritability and mood swings. This emotional change can be scary, so don't be afraid to speak to a female relative about how you're feeling, remember, they've been there too!

I spend ages looking at myself in the mirror and comparing myself to my mates, is this normal?

Of course it is! Puberty causes so many changes, it is hard not to feel self-conscious about your body or compare yourself with others, the important thing is not to get hung up about it. Instead, have fun with your appearance and get to know and love the person you are becoming – you and your body are going to be together for the long haul, so it makes sense to become the best of friends.

ACNE

Spots, blemishes, pimples... no matter what you call them, zits are the pits. Nearly eight out of ten girls will have some form of breakout and you can blame this (and lots of other stuff!) on those pesky hormones. Even though your skin needs a certain amount of oil to keep it supple, during puberty it sometimes produces more than it needs. This can cause your pores to get blocked and create real life, boo-worthy spots.

I've got a big spot on my nose how can I get rid of it?

Your fingertips are home to more pimple-producing oils than you could ever imagine. So no matter how tempting it might be to pop the mini-volcano that's threatening to erupt on your nose – DON'T. This will make it worse causing it to flare up or even worse, to scar the skin. Instead keep the area clean and allow it to disappear in it's own time.

What can I do to help prevent spots?

Make sure you wash your face every day, eat lots of fruit and vegetables and drink lots of toxin-flushing water. It's a myth that chocolate and greasy food cause spots, but eating well will definitely make your skin healthier and less prone to pimples. Spots affect most teens but if you're really bothered about them, speak to your parents and ask them to help you arrange a trip to the docs to get 'em checked out.

BOOBS

One minute there's nothing there and the next there are boob-shaped lumps in your t-shirt, what's going on? Well, your boobs are made up of fatty tissue and milk ducts. As you hit puberty, your nipples will start to change first and gradually you'll notice the area around the nipple getting bigger – these are your boobs and they'll keep growing until you're seventeen or eighteen.

When do I need to get a bra?

As soon as you notice a change in shape, it's a good idea to consider a simple training bra, or sports bra. Most of these come in small, medium, and large. As your boobs get larger you will eventually need something with cups. Cups give you extra support and keep your breasts in place.

Why are mine different to everyone else's?

Every boob-bearing individual has worries about the shape and size of their boobs, and it's common for girls to have one boob bigger than the other. Sometimes this sorts itself out as you get older, but most women will always have slightly different-shaped breasts. Try not to get hung up on the size of your boobs, everyone's are different; they'll always be someone who's bigger or smaller than you.

PUBIC HAIR

One of the most noticeable changes to your body during puberty will be the arrival of extra hair. This normally grows under your armpits and between your legs on your vagina. At first it will appear to be soft, but as it grows it will become thicker and coarser. This is all completely normal, but some girls can feel a little uncomfy about this at first.

Can I get rid of this extra hair?

Some people shave the hair under their arms, so that it doesn't show when they're wearing vests or summer dresses, but it's probably best not to shave between your legs because this can aggravate the sensitive skin down there. Remember, once you shave any body hair, it'll grow back thicker so sometimes it's best just to leave well alone until you're older.

BODY ODOUR

Your sweat glands will become more active during puberty, particularly around the time of your period. This causes extra perspiration, especially under your

arms. When the sweat comes into contact with the air, it dries and goes stale, which means you can end up with a rather unpleasant smell.

What can I do to stop my armpits smelling?

There's nothing you can do about sweat – it's your body's way of regulating your temperature and ensuring that you stay cool. However, you can do something about body odour – have a bath or shower at least once a day and use a deodorant to keep fresh.

What you might notice about lads...

Girls aren't the only ones who go through changes during puberty, y'know…

 BODY SIZE Their arms, legs, hands, and feet may grow faster than the rest of their body. Until the rest of their body catches up, they may feel a little clumsy.

 BODY SHAPE They get taller and their shoulders will get broader.

VOICE Their voice will start cracking and as they continue to grow, it will also become deeper.

HAIR Hair will appear under their arms, on their legs and face, and above their penis. Chest hair may appear during puberty or years after, although not all men have chest hair.

PENIS Their penis and testes will get larger. They may have erections (erections occur when the penis gets stiff and hard) sometimes for no reason. Which can cause major embarrassment for them.

QUIZ: HOW MUCH DO YOU KNOW ABOUT PUBERTY?

Your boobs can be tender, sore and itchy during puberty
True ☐   False ☐

To get rid of body odour you should keep yourself clean and wash under your arms every day
True ☐   False ☐

Any hair that you shave will grow back much thicker
True ☐   False ☐

No two boobs are alike
True ☐   False ☐

Boys are just as self-conscious during puberty as girls
True ☐   False ☐

All these statements are true, if you answered false, go right back and read this section all over again!

A HEALTHY 'TUDE TO FOOD

Get yourself a healthy 'tude to food and you'll feel fabulous inside and out!

❤ If your mood is flatter than a month-old glass of diet coke, your hair and skin are dull or you feel like curling up under the duvet for a week, it's time to show your body some love!

❤ Most of us eat too much of our favourite foods occasionally, but hanging with your gal pals at the local fast-food outlet every night or snacking mindlessly on crisps and chocolate while watching the latest episode of 'Enders, could be doing your body serious damage.

❤ Food, especially bad-for-you food, can be hugely comforting if you're feeling glum, bored or lonely. Now, just 'cause you scoffed a whole pack of biscuits one rainy Sunday, doesn't mean you've harmed your body, but making a habit of it will definitely lead to poor health, lack of fitness and general feelings of ickyness. Not good.

❤ Of course, eating junk food every day won't actually turn you into a bag of greasy chips, but your body – and mind – will feel some serious side effects. When you eat healthy foods with tons of energy and brain-building nutrients you become energetic, clear-thinking and motivated. On the other hand, munching on foods that are low in nutritional value and high in sugar will make you feel sluggish and distracted – what you put in your mouth is more important than you realise.

❤ Making the right eating decisions is quite possibly the nicest thing you can do for yourself, you'll turbo-boost your energy levels and improve your complexion, hair and nails. Anything that makes you feel AND look fabulous has got to be worth a try, right?

Change your 'tude to food by:

❤ Eating breakfast every day. Eating a bowl of cereal, a slice of toast or piece of fruit each morning will stop you reaching for sugary snacks later.

❤ Drinking water, juice, milk or smoothies instead of fizzy drinks. Fizzy drinks are packed with sugar, and the diet type have no nutritional benefits at all.

❤ Drinking 8 glasses of water a day. It flushes out the icky toxins in your body, helps your tummy to work more effectively and hydrates your skin helping to combat bad skin and spots – what's not to love about water?

The odd treat is fine. It really is, you know!

❤ Eat five portions of fruit and veg a day. They'll fill you up and give you all the vits and minerals you need. Even a glass of fruit juice counts!

What is comfort eating?

It's not unusual to eat when you feel sad, angry, bored or lonely, but if you eat in response to your emotions, particularly if you are not hungry, you're comfort eating.

Eating may make you feel better in the short term. Some foods, like chocolate, affect the chemicals in your brain that control your moods. That's why you often feel better straight after you've eaten it, but these effects usually don't last very long.

Comfort eating can be a problem if you are regularly feeling glum and are using food to cope with these feelings.

SIGNS TO LOOK OUT FOR

• Eating quickly

• Eating between meals

• Eating until uncomfortably full

• Eating large amounts of food even though you're not hungry

• Preferring to eat in private

• Feeling depressed or guilty after binging

• Weight gain

If you're eating when you're not hungry and having feelings of guilt it may be a good idea to talk to someone about how you feel and look at other ways of managing them.

Keeping a diary about what you eat and how you feel before and after you eat can help you to see what triggers your eating.

Comfort eating involves eating to help you deal with how you're feeling. You could deal with your feelings in a healthier way by exercising, reading a book or ringing a friend.

HOW HEALTHY ARE YOU?

When you feel hungry, what do you think first?
A. Where's the crisps?
B. I wonder what's in the cupboard?

How often do you have take out?
A. Every week – they're dee-licious!
B. Only as a treat every now and again

Do you eat 5 portions of fruit or veg a day?
A. Er…Not even, is that bad?
B. I do my best!

Before you leave for school, do you always have brekkie?
A. No, I don't have time
B. Yes, I'm hungry first thing

Do you drink plenty of water every day?
A. Nope, water is only for washing my hair in!
B. I forget sometimes but I do try

MOSTLY A'S

Do you know what a piece of fruit actually looks like? While it's fine to eat fast food and chocolate occasionally, you do need to add fresh fruit and veg to your diet. Believe it or not, healthy food can be just as yumsville! You seriously need to work on being a healthier honey!

MOSTLY B'S

You are food sussed! You tend to avoid most junk food and, instead, tuck into super-healthy fruit and veg. You're doing your body one huge massive favour with this approach. Try not to worry if you have the odd bar of chocolate – everyone deserves a treat!

FOOD SWAPS

You don't have to miss out to stay healthy, try swapping your junky snacks for these healthy alternatives.

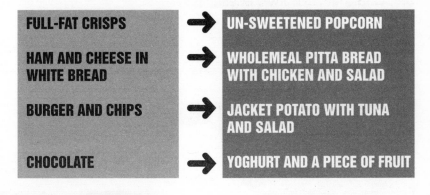

FULL-FAT CRISPS	→	UN-SWEETENED POPCORN
HAM AND CHEESE IN WHITE BREAD	→	WHOLEMEAL PITTA BREAD WITH CHICKEN AND SALAD
BURGER AND CHIPS	→	JACKET POTATO WITH TUNA AND SALAD
CHOCOLATE	→	YOGHURT AND A PIECE OF FRUIT

EAT LIKE A CELEB!

"I drink 8 glasses of water a day and, believe me, I can see a difference. My skin's clearer, I feel healthier and I don't feel sluggish anymore."
Michelle Heaton

"I've learnt to build a normal relationship with both exercise and food. For me, it's not about looking like a supermodel, it's about avoiding junk food, drinking water and feeling good about who I am"
America Ferrera, Ugly Betty

"I drink lots of water to keeps my skin clear and I'm a vegetarian, so I fill up on fruit and veg to make sure I'm always full of energy"
Fearne Cotton, TV presenter

HOW TO EAT YOURSELF HAPPY!

Yes, we've all been told to eat our greens, but there's more to nutritious noshing than digging those sprouts. Here's what to eat, whatever life throws at you.

WHEN YOU WANT TO LOOK GREAT
Orange and red fruit and veggies – berries, peaches, melon, apricots and carrots will make your skin glow. They contain betacarotene, which helps detoxify your body.

WHEN YOU NEED TO BE BRAINY
More Omega-3 fats in your blood = a higher IQ score. How can your body stock up on this brain food? By scoffing certain fish – salmon, herring, mackerel and tuna – and seeds like pumpkin and sunflower.

WHEN YOU NEED TO CHILL
Say 'no' to tea, coffee and cola as the caffeine will make you more edgy. Try green tea, which contains the natural relaxant, theanine.

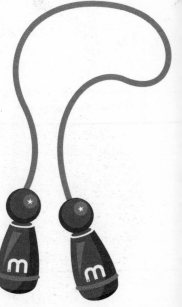

QUIZ: FIND A SPORT YOU LOVE

Want to get fit but don't know where to start? Take our quiz and suss out which exercise excites you.

1 You like to work and play as part of a team.
Yes, go forward 1. No, go forward 2.

2 You like contact play.
Yes, go forward 6. No, go forward 7.

3 You're competitive and enjoy winning.
Yes, go forward 1. No, go forward 2.

4 You'd rather play outdoors.
Yes, go forward 2. No, go forward 3.

5 Think about exercising solo – jogging, swimming, cycling or aerobics are your thing!

6 You want a one-on-one outdoor activity: tennis, running, long-jump.

7 Try one-on-one indoors: squash, kick-boxing, competitive swimming.

8 You're into team sports and don't mind getting bruises: footie, hockey, lacrosse.

9 You want a low-risk group activity: netball, rounders, dancing.

Sweet dreams

Here's how to get a good night's sleep to make sure your body is in tip-top working order...

 Exercise regularly (but not just before bedtime) to de-stress and tire yourself out.

 Develop a bedtime routine – a warm bath and a 20 minute read. You'll subconsciously connect this routine with sleeping and it'll soon help you nod off.

 Go to bed and wake up at the same time every day, including weekends. This will help train your body to sleep.

 Avoid eating too much before bedtime as your bod will be too busy digesting to concentrate on sleep.

Make sure your bedroom is peaceful, quiet and dark – keep it tidy as mess will cause your brain to get stressy. Fill it with sweet smelling, comfortable pillows and cushions.

GETTING FIT = GOOD IDEA; DOING IT = VERY, VERY DULL IDEA.

If you're hopeless at sticking to a keep-fit programme, why not reward yourself each time you exercise? Every time you do 15 minutes of walking, cycling or any other kind of activity, put 20p into a jar. Aim to put at least four coins in every day – walk to school, cycle to the shops, dance to a tune on the radio. You're rewarding yourself as you go. And if you're saving up for those must-have pair of shoes, it's also a great incentive!

Eating healthily, sleeping well and exercising means feeling and looking good. Do you need a better reason?

CHAPTER THREE
FEELING FABULOUS

– yo-yoing between love and heartache & happiness and jealousy? Well it's time to deal with those emotions!

HOW TO BE HAPPY

Makeovers, cute lads, a new album from your favourite band and late-night chats with your gal-pals are all instant happiness fixes, now follow life coach and *mizz* agony aunt, Lisa Clark's tips for a happy life!

BE KIND TO YOURSELF

It's natural to feel a bit sad now and again. But don't give yourself a hard time about it. Some things can help you feel better almost straight away. Try a brisk walk or write down your worries. You could even try wearing a bright colour like pink, orange or yellow – it'll rub off on your mood and give you an instant lift.

SEE THE UPSIDE

Every situation has one. Been dumped by your crush? Well, in between crying fits and eating chocolate, remind yourself you're better off without him. At least this way, you're free for the next foxy lad who crosses your path.

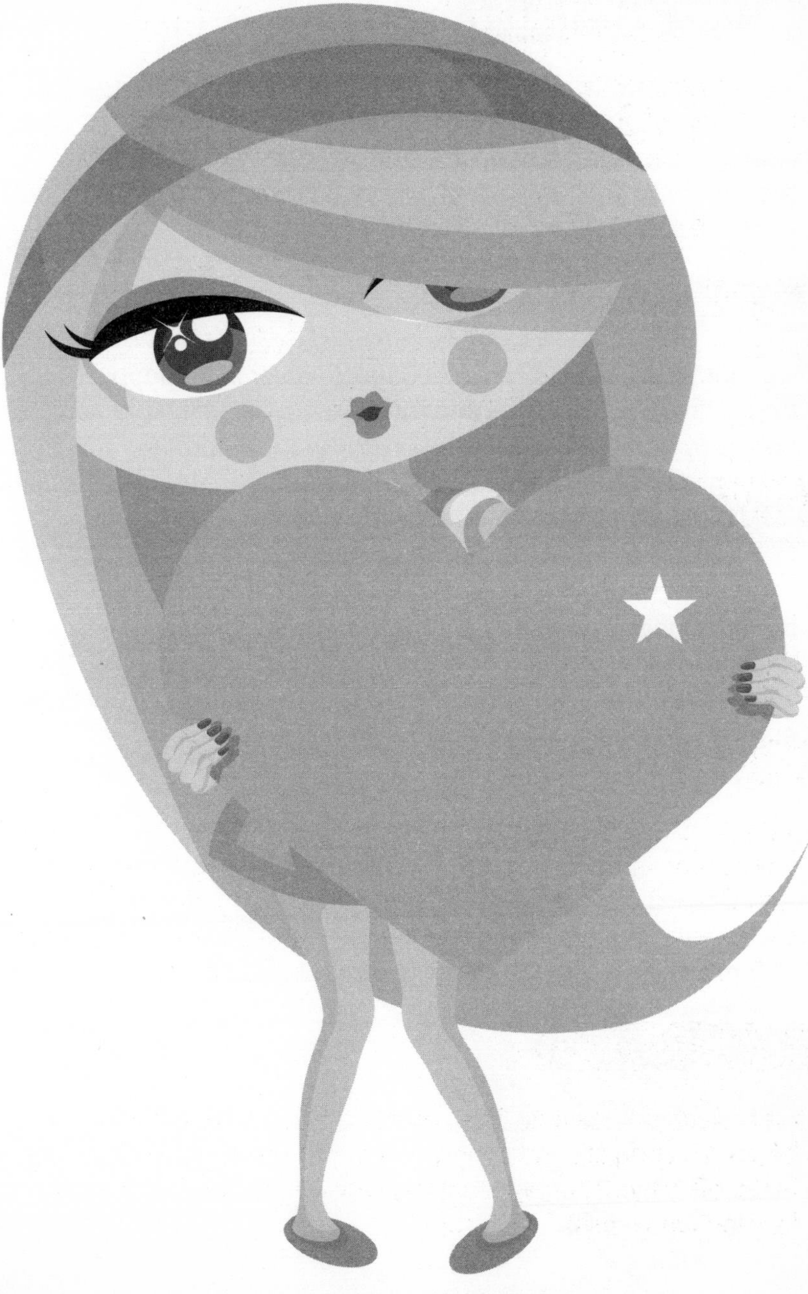

BELIEVE IN YOURSELF

There's no such word as 'can't' and if you remember that, you'll be able to do just about anything. For others to believe in you, you need to believe in yourself first. And you can't expect people to like you if you don't even like yourself! So take a deep breath and have a can-do attitude at all times.

NO COMPARISON

You don't have to be skinnier/smarter/funnier to be happy. Concentrate on the things that make you awesome, right here, right now and celebrate those – insta-happy thoughts!

LIVE THE DREAM

Resolve to do something out of the ordinary at least once every month. It doesn't need to be a huge thing like jumping out of a plane or swimming with dolphins, but trying new things will make you feel alive and exhilarated. Don't just daydream, get out there and do something cool. Today!

Banish the blush

Have you ever wanted the ground to open up and swallow you whole? Do you dread your teacher asking you a question in class? Do you break out in a hot flush at the sight of your boy crush?

If you're totally timid, get easily embarrassed and your blushes flash like a neon sign without your permission – it's time to wave bye-bye to lil' miss shy and banish the blushes for good!

WHAT IS SHYNESS?

Shyness tends to strike in certain kinds of social situations – like the first day of school, when you're meeting someone new, striking up a conversation with someone you feel attracted to, or giving a presentation in class. You're more likely to feel shy and at risk of an attack of the blushes when you're not sure what will happen, how others will react, or when all eyes are on you.

CRINGE!

A cringe-worthy moment can have exactly the same effect. Think turning up to a party in fancy dress only to find it's not actually fancy dress or walking into a glass door because you thought it was open.

TOTAL RED-FACED, MORTIFICATION, RIGHT?

Now, while you may want to run in the opposite direction or go dive under your duvet for quite possibly the rest of your life, neither are actually a do-able option, which is why we blush in embarrassment instead!

SO WHY DO OUR CHEEKS GO RED, EXACTLY?

Well, when you're faced with something that might make you blush, like, bumping into your cute boy-crush or speaking in front of the entire class, our heart beats faster and you may find you're breathing quicker than usual. Our bodies go into shock and don't know whether to see the situation through or get up and leave quick-smart. So, to try and get us moving, blood rushes to our muscles to make them faster and stronger. Some of this blood goes to our face and that is why we turn tomato red.

5 STEPS TO BUSTING THE BLUSH!

If you find yourself in a blush-some situation, don't panic, here is our 5-step guide...

1. SMILE

❤ So what if you got your hair stuck in the zipper of a top in the changing room?

❤ So what if the snotty assistant had to help you out?

❤ Don't cringe indefinitely, just smile at her and laugh it off.

While it may be easier said than done, laughing it off is most definitely the best thing to do. You've got to laugh about it – because when you laugh, the world will laugh with you and let's face it, there really is nothing more attractive than a girl who knows how to laugh.

2. ACT UP

❤ If you trip over your words when talking to the cute boy in your maths class or find yourself wearing the exact same outfit as your best gal pal – don't stess, just stand tall and do as we do, ask yourself what your favourite movie star would do?

❤ If ever we find ourselves in a potential blush-like sitch, we ask: "what would Ashley Tisdale do?"

If she turned up to a celeb party wearing the same outfit as her co-star, we bet she would simply smile and brush off any feelings of embarrassment, pronto. So, make like your fave movie star, and act confident, no matter what the situation. That way you'll get away with practically anything!

3. BE SILLY

♥ Don't take yourself too seriously.

Okay, so you've walked into class and your skirt is tucked in your Paul Frank knickers, instead of running in the opposite direction, simply throw your classmates a cheeky wink and do a li'l happy dance. Oh, and then un-tuck them, obviously.

4. LOVE YOURSELF UP

♥ If you're still cringing from the shame of letting out a bottom burp in front of your best bud and her family – don't. Remind yourself that it has probably happened to them too.

Beating yourself up about it is gonna get you nowhere, so just forget about it! Instead, collect compliments – write 'em down in a cute little journal and you can flick back anytime you need to remind yourself how totally fabulous you are.

5. THINK POSITIVE!

If, after an embarrassing incident you're thinking: "what a total idiot jeez, I'm so dumb!" flick your negative thinking switch to 'positive' and say this instead: "It could have been a whole lot worse, it's not such a big deal!"

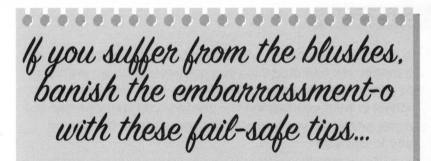

If you suffer from the blushes, banish the embarrassment-o with these fail-safe tips...

STAY CALM When your cheeks threaten an attack of the 'hot reds', breathe big, deep breaths and whatever the situation, don't stress. If you're having a blush-worthy moment – just chill.

LAUGH IT UP So what if you broke the chair in the science lab? So what if you accidentally said a rude word in a class presentation? Just shrug your shoulders and laugh it up, because when you laugh, the world laughs with you!

DON'T THINK ABOUT IT Next time you feel your cheeks burning up, switch your thoughts to something totally dullsville instead, like a math sum or your geography homework. Before you know it, your blushes will have totally faded.

BE DISTRACT -O GIRL The next time you find yourself feeling mucho embarrassed, distract the people you're with by changing the subject. If everyone sees you acting like you're not bothered, well, they won't care either – hurrah!

STRESS SOS

Is your diary so packed with things-to-do that just looking at it makes you feel dizzy? Do you put yourself under pressure to perform well in exams? Are you too busy worrying about others to treat yourself like the princess you undoubtedly are? If you answered yes to any of these questions, it's time for you to chill out!

WHAT IS STRESS?

❤ Unfortunately, stress is an unavoidable part of life. School demands, changes in your body, problems with your friends, arguments with your family, changing schools or taking on too much, are the most common stressors and can leave you feeling stranded in a sea of tension.

❤ Not all stress is bad – some stress is good. In fact, everyone needs a little bit of stress in their lives; it's what kicks your butt out of bed in the morning, makes you feel better on exams and gives you the confidence boost to ask out your boy crush. In other words, good stress gets your heart pumping, ups your breathing rate and causes chemical reactions throughout your body.

❤ The problems occur, however, when stress becomes excessive. It can become destructive and turn into distress, and too much stress on your mind and body can make you feel miserable, worried, sad and ill.

You know you're stressed when...

 You find it difficult to sleep and you're tossing and turning at 3am

 You're eating three chocolate bars in a row or not eating at all

 You're irritable, snappy and short-tempered

 Concentrating becomes very difficult

 You think about homework and feel overwhelmed

 You start listing all the negative things that get you down

STRESS: BUSTED!

How to handle your most stressful situations...

I get so worried about homework that I panic and end up getting nothing done.

STRESS BUSTER! Break it down! Make a list of exactly what work you have, then assign a time slot for each class subject. Be sure you schedule a few minutes between sessions for study breaks – everyone needs to step away once in a while. This way your tasks will become more manageable.

If I could change my belly/nose/freckles/bum I'd be happier.

STRESS BUSTER! Instead of getting hung up on the stuff you can't change, pick your best features and maximize them. Then remind yourself of them often (as in "I love my curves" or "I love the way my eyebrows frame my face"). When you like one thing about yourself, chances are, you'll soon start to love the rest of you, too.

I don't know how to talk to boys. I get too nervous and I don't know what to say.

STRESS BUSTER! Remember, guys are people too – even your dream guy is a regular person, honest! When you get to know boys as friends and not just crushes, talking to them isn't so scary. Find out what you have in common and use it to start a conversation. Hey, you'll be surprised to discover boys like it when girls are real.

I hate fighting with my parents.

STRESS BUSTER! If you and your parents are arguing, you can probably put it down to nomal teen vs. parent battles – they happen in almost every home. If you think your mum or dad are being unfair, then talk to them. But you have to listen to what they say as well. A little communication can relieve a lot of tension. Dishing out the silent treatment is a sure fire ticket to stressville. Talk, talk, talk!

CHILL, BABY!

Banish panic with these fabulous chill-out techniques...

GET PHYSICAL: exercise is an easy way to get those happy hormones pumping. If sports or fitness classes aren't your thing, simply shut your bedroom door and rock out to your favourite feel-good tunes.

LAUGH-OUT-LOUD: laughing is a great way to relieve stress and get rid of negative thoughts. Find the things that make you laugh out loud, like funny DVDs, for whenever you need a giggle boost.

TURN OFF: flick the 'off' switch in your head for at least 10 minutes. Lie back on your bed and do absolutely nothing except relax, starting with your head all the way down to your tippy-toes – bliss.

SMILE: the act of smiling, even when you don't feel like it, can lift your mood in a second. Try it!

HAVE FUN: doing stuff you love, like reading, painting, shopping, hanging out with your friends, is the ultimate destressor.

TOTAL DE-STRESS
For you and your bezzies

Pamper party – There's nothing more relaxing and fun than getting all your buds over for a night of pamper-lishous fun! Organise a weekend sleepover packed with facials, manicures, pedicures and scrummy snacks. No boys allowed!

DVD fest – Girl and boy mates can bring over their fave DVDs. Decide the playlist, make the popcorn and chill out. It can be a real laugh watching movies you'd never normally watch and all voting on the best and worst of the night.

Family funday – Get the whole family to relax by getting them together and having a giggle. Go bowling, go to an exhibition, go on a picnic, have a Wii tournament – whatever! Your folks could probably do with some wind down time too.

HOW TO ARGUE - AND WIN EVERY TIME

THE SEVEN RULES OF COMBAT

1 **LISTEN** It's important to know where they're coming from so you can argue back with skill.

2 **MIMIC** Watch their body language and subtly copy what they're doing, and match the speed they speak at. It will send them a subconscious message that you're on the same wavelength.

3 **MAKE EYE-CONTACT** This shows you're interested in their point of view.

4 **USE THEIR LANGUAGE** Are they visual people (saying things like "I see what you mean"), kinesthetic (using emotional language like "I feel the same") or auditory ("Sounds good to me")? Work it out then use the same lingo.

5 **HOLD YOUR TEMPER** Flying off the handle never solved anything. If you feel yourself losing it, say, "Sorry, I'm getting angry" and take a minute to calm down.

6 **DON'T MAKE IT PERSONAL** Turning an argument into a barrage of criticism is not good. Avoid starting sentences with "You…", blaming them for the problem. Instead try "I feel you…" – it shows you accept responsibility for half the problem.

7 **STICK TO THE POINT** Focus on what you're arguing about. Don't go off on tangents about everything else they do wrong.

How to deal with people when they annoy you...

MUM
: Listen to her, she might actually have something valid to say – she's not a fool just because she's your mum. Don't assume, without evidence, that she's trying to run your life.

TEACHER
: A teacher doesn't expect you to argue back as their job is based on the idea that they know best. Stay respectful in any argument and keep your voice low and calm to show this.

BOYFRIEND
: Be aware that he's going to assume that you're being emotional. Your aim is to prove that you're not – so don't get upset and lose your temper, no matter how tempting.

FRIEND
: The idea of arguing with their best friend makes most girls feel uncomfy. So approach a disagreement as a difference of opinion, not an argument – and know when to compromise.

HOW FABULOUS DO YOU FEEL?

Do you glance in shop windows to check your appearance?
A. Now and again, I try to look my best.
B. Hardly ever, it makes me feel down.

If someone gives you a compliment, how do you feel?
A. Feel a bit awkward but secretly pleased.
B. Embarrassed, they're probably just being nice.

How do you compare to the rest of your gang?
A. Ok, we're all pretty much the same.
B. I'm the ugly duckling.

Do you envy the lives and looks of celebs?
A. Not really, they're gorgeous but it's not all real.
B. All the time – how are you meant to live up to them?

Your crush smiles at you, do you:
A. Smile and hope he comes over to talk to you.
B. Look behind you to see who he's really checking out.

MOSTLY A'S

You're a walking talking example of fabulousness! You appreciate your good points, look on the positive side of life and feel happy in your own skin. People enjoy your company and lads find you easy to talk to as you're not one to put yourself down. You should help others to feel good about themselves too!

MOSTLY B'S

You're suffering a bit of low self-esteem. Flick through the 'Feeling Fabulous' chapter again and lose the blues. Come on, you're as gorgeous, smart and funny as the next girl, you just haven't learned how to use your charms. Time to see the glass as half full rather than half empty. Think fabulous, be fabulous!

Don't get hung up on the things you can't change, pick your best features and maximize them.

54

CHAPTER FOUR
WE ARE FAMILY
– irritating brothers, step families and overprotective families – sorted.

SIBLINGS: SUSSED

Got a nightmare of a brother? Or a sister who's just too perfect for words? Although it might seem like your siblings are your worst enemies, if you learn to get along, you might actually become mates! So get sib-sussed..

SHE'S MISS POPULAR

Your older sister is so amazing. Gorgeous, popular, great sense of style – to you, she's got it all. She always dresses on trend, never gets a spot and has all the lads chasing after her. One look at her makes you really aware of all the things you don't like about yourself.

SIB-SUSSED! Firstly, chill out. Yes, your sis may seem to have it all, but chances are she's just as paranoid as us normal girls. No one is immune from worrying about their looks – even the most beautiful models and celebrities have parts of their bodies they'd like to change. Secondly, being gorgeous doesn't have to mean being like her. Instead learn to accept that everyone is different, and to appreciate all the things that make you uniquely you! Share your worries with her – she'll probably laugh and tell you how much she hates her big feet or slightly wonky teeth! Then, maybe she'll help you to find which clothes, hairstyles and make-up suit you best, so you can look fab without feeling the need to be a clone of her.

HE'S A HEADACHE

You and your older brother used to have a right laugh together, but over the last few months, he's just been impossible. He's sulky, difficult and picks so many arguments it ruins the atmosphere at home. Now you actually hate it when he's around.

SIB-SUSSED! It could be that he's going through puberty – and the hormones that control it can play havoc with even the sunniest personality. As well as giving him body changes to get used to – facial hair, a breaking voice, long, clumsy limbs and zits – they can also cause extreme mood swings. Remember too, that while girls tend to burst into tears and talk about their issues with their mates, lads are more likely to get angry and bottle up their worries. He should get through this and become more like his old self again, given a bit of time and space. But, if you're concerned that there's more to it, or just want to let him know that you care, try talking to him when he's in a more bearable mood. And if he still snaps at you, try not to take it so personally!

Parents – how to deal

Over-protective parents

★ **Are you desperate for freedom? Your best bet is to show your mum and dad how grown-up and responsible you are. That way, they're more likely to cut you some slack. Offer to do the washing up, put out the rubbish without being asked. Once your parents see how eager you are to prove yourself, they might loosen up.**

★ Remember: Rome wasn't built in a day, so don't expect too much too soon. See every ounce of independence gained as a major victory.

Favourites

★ **No matter what you think or feel, your parents don't**

have favourites among their children. They may get on better with one or the other of you at any given time, or find one easier than another to deal with, but they do love you all the same.

★ If you're feeling left out, why not suggest to your mum or dad that you do something together which doesn't involve any of your brothers and sisters. That way they'll get the hint that you're feeling a bit neglected and will try their best to do something about it.

Being part of a step-family

★ **Remember you are one of 18 million people in the UK living in a step-family. So you're not alone. Try to bear this in mind if you feel it hard explaining your family situation to other people. You're bound to find someone in the same boat as you.**

★ No one expects you to love your new step-parents straight off. You may not even like them, and it's quite natural to have these feelings. These relationships take time, so give living together a go and try to talk about the situation as much as possible.

★ Try confiding in someone outside your immediate family who can act as a negotiator and a friendly ear. Lean on your mates too, they're always a good source of support, you just need to let them know what you need.

TAME YOUR TEMPER

Families can drive you to distraction, but if you often get so crazy-angry that you totally lose it, it's time to learn how to cool it, hothead!

Whether it's your little bro slamming the bathroom door in your face your mum saying you can't stay out later than nine, things happen which upset us. Sometimes it can get so bad we think we're going to explode and we end up yelling or lashing out at anyone that gets in our way. If this sounds like you, it's time to tame your temper.

TEMPER, TEMPER

★ **So you've thrown a hissy fit of monumental proportions. You told your mum exactly what you think of her and stomped off to your room slamming every door behind you, feel better? Maybe for five minutes, but how long is it 'til you start thinking 'how long do I have to spend sulking before I can face her again?'**

The problem is, when you get red-faced and angry, you lose the ability to think logically. You're so crazy-mad and annoyed that even if a cute boy walked in the room you wouldn't notice! Losing your temper can mean losing the argument too, even if you were right. Not only do you feel daft, the chances are you'll look pretty daft too, which means the person you're angry with will end up all pleased and smug-faced, which will then make you angry all over again.

Kicking off every time something upsets you is going to seriously stress you out, so instead of turning red with rage and sending out 'I-want-hassle' signals, turn your temper switch to 'cool' and count to ten…

THE ANGRY ANNIE

"...I've been really angry lately. I constantly find myself getting annoyed with my mates and my family. I don't say anything but I can feel the anger bubbling up inside me..."

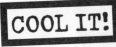

Keeping anger inside like this can really mess with your health. So, next time, instead of bottling it up or shouting your mouth off, try walking around the block a few times or going up to your room 'til you no longer feel like a time bomb waiting to go off. Then, try and go back to dealing with the situation again – calmly this time.

LIL' MISS STROPPY

"...I've started getting really stroppy. Everything seems completely unfair if it doesn't go my way, so I'll shout until it does..."

If you've got a case of 'me, me, me' syndrome, the only way to deal with this situation is to start changing your ways and make a real effort to put others first. Begin by sharing your Mp3 player with a mate on the way to school, offer someone else

the last seat on the bus, or buy a pack of sweets for your sis as well as yourself. You'll be surprised how good it makes you feel.

THE MOODY 'MARE

"...I've been feeling really depressed and I just don't know what to do, I shout at my sister and then cry for no reason..."

 If you find yourself feeling energetic and positive one minute, then totally narky the next, blame your hormones. These monster mood swings are because us girls have so many crazy hormones pumping around our bodies that our brains have a seriously hard time keeping up with all the changes. Help deal with it by talking out angry feelings, and let off steam by dancing, running or playing some loud music.

TEMPER TAMERS

Keep your calm with these 'cool it, girl' temper tamers.

Don't wind yourself up The worst thing you can do is think negative thoughts like 'they all hate me' or 'they think I'm an idiot'. When you hold on to bitterness it stays with you and makes you zilcho fun to be around — whatever's happened has happened and you can't change it. Focus on everything positive that happens instead, keep a diary and you'll have an instant reminder of how fab things can be.

Recognise your feelings Know your tell-tale anger signs as soon as they start. Then, whenever you notice that 'red heat' rising, you'll be able to stop yourself. Tell whoever is upsetting you that you don't want to talk right now, as it'll only make you angry and walk away.

Cool off Take time away from the person or situation that is making you angry. Once you're on your own, take deep breaths, listen to your favourite music or watch a funny DVD. Do whatever it takes to calm you down. Once you've cooled off, go back to the person who made you angry and say you'd like to discuss the problem. Then sit down and talk about it as calmly as you can. You'll feel better once it has been sorted.

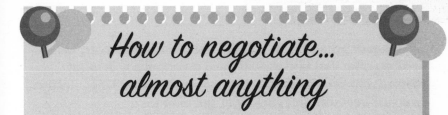

How to negotiate...
almost anything

Remember: Make the ABC work for you:

ANTECEDENTS – BEHAVIOUR – CONSEQUENCES

If you're worked up about getting what you want and have already decided your parents won't agree…

…you're likely to be aggressive towards them, and they'll shout back and nobody wants to listen…

Result? You don't get your own way and you're miserable. Nothing achieved.

To change the Consequences you need to change A or B. So…

A. Don't make it a big deal
B. Ask your parents "What do I need to do to get this outcome?"

COPING WITH DIVORCE

When your parents split up they will usually both carry on looking after you and should have an equal say in what happens to you. It's vital to remember they won't stop loving you just because they no longer get along.

What you need to know

♥ They may need to go to court to decide what's going to happen. The court will put your welfare first and you should have a chance to tell them what you would like to happen, but if you don't want to, you don't have to.

♥ Don't allow your parents to draw you into taking sides. This can be really difficult and confusing but try to stay out of their battles.

♥ Don't feel guilty about letting your parents both know how you're feeling. They're probably both so caught up in what's going on that they may need a little reminder.

♥ Don't feel like you have to please both parents all the time, but equally don't try to blackmail them or play them off against each other.

♥ Realise that you're not alone. There are thousands of girls in your situation, so it might help to find/make a friend who is going through the same thing. As with all difficult situations talking and sharing will help you manage the hard times. You can also help others.

♥ Make sure you chat about your intimate feelings and thoughts as this will lift the burden from you but if you feel you can't cope, you can call Childline in complete confidence on 0800 1111

You can call Childline on 0800 1111

FAMILY AFFAIRS

Are you laid-back about your family, or do they always wind you up? Take this tolerance test to find out...

ANSWER YES OR NO

1. Are you proud to be seen out with your family?
2. Do you get on well with your folks?
3. Are you mates with your brothers and/or sisters?
4. Do you love big family parties?
5. Do you like having friends round for tea?
6. You can't imagine ever leaving home.

MAINLY NO'S
Family misfortunes!

Oh dear! You find your nearest and dearest very embarrassing to be around, and would rather hang out with your mates than your family. You put up with them, but they irritate you and make you cringe, so it's not easy. Try not to be so hard on them though – perhaps you just need to make a bit more effort to find out what makes them tick, you never know, with a bit of effort, you might just find out they're OK!

MAINLY YES'S
Happy Families

You're more than happy to spend time with your family, and you have as much fun with them as you do with your girl gang. Your mates envy your close relationship with your parents, but you've sussed that it's better to stay friends with your folks than to constantly disagree with them. That way, they treat you like more of a grown-up, and that can only have heaps of positive benefits! ABC sussed!

FAMILY TREE

What role do you play in your family?
Answer yes or no to find out...

ANSWER YES OR NO

1. I'm the one everyone comes to for a moan!
2. I like to let everyone else do the talking.
3. I'm not treated like the baby.
4. My folks give me lots of freedom.
5. I don't like to be the centre of attention.
6. I feel that I have too much responsibility sometimes.

MAINLY NO'S
Kid sis!
Whatever your place in the family line-up, you always want to be the family pet, the baby of the pack. You like to be indulged and spoiled by your folks and sibs, but you're also good at keeping the peace and making sure that everyone is getting on well. You have a very caring nature, so make sure you are as good to your relatives as they are to you!

MAINLY YES'S
Big sis!
Even if you're not the eldest child in your family, your siblings look up to you because you're a cool role model. You're a great listener and always have time for whoever wants to chat – or to have a good old whinge! Just make sure you make plenty of lil' ol' me-time, and don't be afraid to tell your folks that you feel a bit of pressure now and then.

CHAPTER FIVE
BE-THERE BUDS
YOU + GOOD FRIENDS
= *happy times!*

FIND FRIENDS FAST!

Great girl buds are just like shoes; you can never have too many, so say goodbye to lil' miss shy and follow our guide to finding fab friends fast!

GET OUT THERE

The only people you're going to meet sat in front of the TV each night is the cast of your favourite soap, so to meet new people outside of school, you've gotta get out there, girl! Whether you're a sport star or an art girl, no matter what you're into, there's guaranteed to be a club you can join or something at your local youth centre that will float your boat, with members your age. Not only will you get to learn new skills, there's the added bonus of hanging with people who have similar interests to you. Remember that the nerves will only last the first time, each time you go you will gain in confidence. If you can, find a friend that will go with you so you feel more confident and that way you can both make new mates.

BUD-MAKIN' ACTION

Grab the yellow pages or ask for info at your local library about the clubs and activities available in your local area.

BE OPEN MINDED

Okay, so the girl who lives two doors down with the really cute hand-made skirt/bag combo is a year younger than you, who cares? Don't write off a possible fab friendship just because you think you won't get on. Whether someone wears goth-like make-up or carries a fluffy pink handbag, don't be afraid to approach them. By being open minded about your new hang-out girls, not only will you bag a new bud, you could discover your new favourite band or get the chance to pick up some super-cool customising tips.

BUD-MAKIN' ACTION

If there's a girl in your area who seems cool and is someone you think you'd like to hang out with, then approach her. It could end up with a friendship that lasts way beyond the hols.

DON'T BE SHY

If you don't talk to new people, then how are they ever going to find out what a great person you are? Approaching new people can be super-scary but with a little bit of practise, you will soon become a confident fab friend-making queen!

Every girl loves a compliment, right? So if someone is wearing a pair of shoes that you really like, tell them that you're digging their footwear and that you were wondering where they got them from. Not only will the person be super-flattered, they'll also know you're a girl of impeccable taste who they will want to be friends with! Or, if you hear someone talking about your favourite band or a film you've just seen, don't interrupt a conversation, but don't be afraid to show an interest and offer a new perspective. Before you know it you'll be nattering for hours!

BUD-MAKIN' ACTION

Smile, make eye contact and introduce yourself. You will become instantly approachable and people will be queuing to hang out with you.

MAKING CONVERSATION

It's good to talk but when you're making new friends it can sometimes be difficult to know what to say. Chill out! The more you stress about it, the harder it'll become. Start by giving off positive signals to your soon-to-be friend by making eye contact when you talk and standing with your hands by your side – you'll seem chilled and mega-friendly. Then, make sure that when you speak to someone for the first time, no matter how nervous you might be, try not to spend the whole conversation talking about you. Without being super nosey, ask them questions about themselves. Make sure you listen, too. Finding out about people and their lives, is half the fun of making new friends! People are also naturally drawn to those that seem interested in them.

BUD-MAKIN' ACTION

Don't just ask questions that have a yes/no answer Instead try things like, 'that's a cool belt, where's it from?' or 'what did you think of Eastenders last night?' That way it'll keep the conversation going and encourage her to shoot questions back at you – voilà, instant friends!

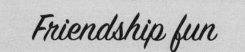

Friendship fun

If you and your new buds are stuck for ideas of what to do, check these out...

★ Go the park - take a picnic, a big blanket, sunblock and a frisbee. Add new fab friends and you have a free, insta-girl gathering!

★ For a rainy day embrace your inner geeks and have a board game tournament — you know you'll love it! Loser buys the ice creams!

★ Become art girls and journal your fun by logging onto www.fotolog.com and taking a photo each day. Day 1: Frisbee throwing snaps. Day 2: You in your brand new trainers. Day 3: The hot guy you're crushing on. These are the things you'll want to remember.

★ Have a sand castle building competition. Don't live near a beach? Hijack your lil' sister's sandbox — summer is about getting creative! For inspiration check out: www.sandcastlecentral.com

★ Host the ultimate DVD-athon — you may want to make this a three day event depending on the weather — Our picks: *Mean Girls*, *Clueless*, *Legally Blonde*.

IS YOUR MATE A COPY CAT?

Is your pal a walking, talking cookie-cutter version of you? Does your best bud copy your style, your hair-cut or even your taste in music? If you've got a friend who has trouble thinking for herself there's a chance she may have a serious case of the Copy-cat. Don't worry though, we've got the cure!

COPY-CAT FRIENDS

From emulating celebrities we admire, to buying a 'cool' pair of jeans just because the so-called popular girls all have them, we've all copied from the people around us sometimes. In fact, when it comes to friendships, copying can be one of the main ways we compliment or show our friends that we rate their look and style. But it doesn't mean it's always welcome!

WANNA BE LIKE YOUR GAL PAL?

Believe it or not, copying our gal pals is actually a normal part of being a girl in the world. For example, if you find yourself in a really awkward situation, you may look to your more experienced friends for info on what you should or shouldn't do. If a friend has qualities that you like and admire – maybe she's really confident or knows how to charm teachers with a killer-watt smile – you may copy her in the hope of sharing those qualities. Finally, if you copy what your friends wear, think, or say, it may help you feel like you're actually fitting in.

Take the so-called popular girls in your school – when a group is seen as popular, people like to associate themselves with that group, right? The girls in the gang will dress a certain way and do their hair in a certain style to make sure everyone knows they're part of the so-called popular group. Why?

BECAUSE WE COPY PEOPLE THAT WE ADMIRE AND IT SHOWS THAT WE WANT TO BE LIKE THEM. HOWEVER, IT'S SO MUCH COOLER TO BE UNIQUE!

WHAT TO DO WHEN SOMEONE COPIES YOU...

If one day you're rocking a hot-pink beret and matching scarf and the next day your bestie is working an identical ensemble, it can be flattering at first. But if your friend is working your entire wardrobe by the end of the week, and she keeps turning up in the same gear it can be extremely irritating.

While it's kind of flattering when a gal-pal wants to look and dress like you, if this becomes a serious case of the copy-cats, your uniqueness will become threatened and it may ruin your friendship.

IF THIS SOUNDS LIKE YOUR FRIEND...

♥ If she wants to look like you, there's a good chance she's suffering from low self-esteem. When people don't feel confident they sometimes think that looking like someone else will help them to fit in. Why not plan a girl's night in and flick through copies of *mizz* – encourage her to point out things she likes and show her things you think might suit her. Helping her to develop her own unique style will not only boost her self-esteem but will stop her from copying yours.

When people don't feel confident they might think that looking like someone else will help them fit in.

♥ If there are days when she's not copying your look – be sure to compliment her. She may not have enough confidence to experiment with her look and decides to play it safe by copying you. If you see her wearing something different or working a new hair cut – tell her how great it looks. Once she has proof she can do it alone, she won't want to copy you anymore.

♥ If her copy-cat behaviour is really getting you down, then it's time to let her know. It might be tough at first, but it's a good idea to express your feelings about it early on. You don't have to be harsh, but you do have to be honest.

PRETTY YOU-NIQUE

It's totally cool to be inspired by celebrities, movie stars, people we meet and our gal-pals, we can discover a lot about what we like from films, TV and magazines and from each others styles. In fact, it's one of the main ways we learn. But instead of trying to work a body shape that's just not healthy or saving up for months on end to own a super-expensive designer bag, take a look in the mirror.

WHAT MAKES YOU STAND OUT FROM THE CROWD? WHAT MAKES YOU SO FABULOUSLY DIFFERENT TO EVERYONE ELSE? EXPERIMENT WITH WHAT'S IN YOUR WARDROBE TO CREATE A LOOK THAT'S COMPLETELY YOU-SHAPED.

BEZZIE BICKERING

Even the closest friends fall out now and again. Arguments are upseting but what's really important is how you sort it out. Speak to your mate about what's happened...

DO...

✓ Sit down and discuss any issues calmly and rationally.

✓ Explain your side of the argument and let her explain her side.

✓ Apologise if it was your fault, or accept her apology if she offers one.

✓ Be reasonable. Understand, compromise and agree to differ if need be.

✓ Let it drop once it has been resolved.

DON'T...

✗ Shout, accuse, or insult. It all just leads to bad feeling.

✗ Butt in, argue back or shout her down while she's trying to talk.

✗ Let pride get in the way of you both sorting the problem out quickly.

✗ Be stubborn; make time to talk.

✗ Continue the quarrel for weeks on end.

TOXIC FRIENDS

Could your best mate be poisoning your friendship with her bad behaviour?

She puts you down with her nasty one-liners, she laughs at you for crushin' on the cute one from your favourite boyband and she 'accidentally' spills your best-kept secrets - with a friend like this, who needs enemies? Avoid a bitch-fest by identifying your poison pals, pronto.

If your gal pal is intent on being a major friendship killer, here's how to deal with her toxic traits.

SHE'S JEALOUS

Few things are worse than a mate who's got a case of the green-eyed monster. Whether it's over your grades being better than hers or you getting a cool new outfit when she can't afford one, she always makes you feel bad.

SHE'LL SAY... "I don't know what you see in that boy – he's a total geek."

HOW TO DEAL Try and understand how she's feeling. If she's skint it must be tough to see you in cool new clothes. And if she's been left out while you're spending time with a new boy she's bound to feel hurt. Acting like she didn't want them in the first place is her way of making herself feel better. Why not make time to see her, and try and see past the negative comments.

SHE PUTS YOU DOWN

It's funny, but you always end up feeling stupid around her. With your other friends, you never feel like that, but with her snide comments and constant put-downs, she always has you feeling like a major fool.

SHE'LL SAY... "Why do you want straightening irons? They'll make your hair look even worse."

HOW TO DEAL This gal pal gets her kicks by making your life a misery with her constant put-downs, and while it may be tempting to throw a mouthful of abuse right back at her, instead ask for a quiet word. Explain to her how bad it makes you feel when she disses you. Tell her you don't think it's a joke – none of what she says makes you laugh. If she doesn't get it, you might want to consider distancing yourself from her for a bit. When she realises you're serious, she'll probably come running back to you. However, if her comments become worse and she steps over the line, she is getting close to becoming a bully. Do not stand for bullying in any form. If you feel that you cannot handle it alone, tell a trusted adult and get some help and support. Do not suffer in silence.

SHE'S SO POSSESSIVE

You like her, but she won't give you a minute's peace. Mention you're eating lunch with the new girl and she'll insist on tagging along, if you tell her you met up with another friend at the weekend, she'll sulk and make you feel bad about it. She makes you feel guilty all the time and it's getting you down.

SHE'LL SAY... "Why are you going off without me? Don't you want me to come with you?"

HOW TO DEAL You've got to be firm. Gently explain that you really like her and she's a great mate – but you like to have other mates too. You don't always have to invite her and there's nothing to feel guilty about. Why not invite her along the next time you're seeing a bunch of your mates? That way she can start making more friends of her own and you won't feel as though she's trying to hang out with just you. Try and be sensitive to her feelings as she may find it hard to socialise and she might only feel comfortable with you.

SHE SPILLS SECRETS

Oh no. You told your mate your biggest secret – and now everyone knows. It can only have come from her. She's been gossiping about you with the others and you're really hurt.

SHE'LL SAY... "I didn't tell anyone, honest."

HOW TO DEAL It could just be that she can't help herself and thinks by sharing gossip with others, people will like her more. If you think that this is the case, then it's down to you to be more careful who you share your must-keep secrets with in future. If she's doing it to stir trouble, like Regina from the film Mean Girls, this is truly toxic behaviour, and the best way to avoid getting caught up in her war of words is to just stay clear of her.

CHECK BOX QUIZ
Is she toxic?

Find out if your friendship is on the right track – or if you should end it.

SHE ROCKS IF...

If you check three or more, your friend is most definitely a keeper.

 SHE REACHES OUT: she calls, texts and wants to hang out as often as you do.

 SHE'S SUPPORTIVE: she gives advice when you ask for it and lets you rant without interrupting.

SHE BOOSTS YOUR EGO: she lets you know why she likes you, so you feel good about yourself.

 SHE SHARES WITH YOU: not just shoes, she wants to know about your life – and she wants to tell you about hers.

SHE'S DIRECT: she tells you when she's angry or upset, instead of getting a mood on and giving you the silent treatment without explaining why.

✓ **SHE RESPECTS YOU:** she knows what you like and what you believe – and doesn't judge you because of it.

SHE SUCKS IF...

If you check any of these – go check our 'What to Do' tips now...

 SHE HOLDS BACK: you call, IM, and invite her out – but she doesn't really do the same with you.

 SHE JUDGES YOU: she criticises your choices before you get a chance to explain.

 SHE UNDERMINES YOU: she often brings up your insecurities, so you often doubt yourself when you're around her.

 SHE'S SELF-ABSORBED: somehow your conversations always seem to be about her.

 SHE BLOWS YOU OUT: you can't take plans with her seriously as she ends up cancelling them.

✓ **SHE'S SELF-DESTRUCTIVE:** you worry she might drag you into her reckless behaviour, like smoking or drinking.

WHAT TO DO

The best way to deal with a potential friendship killer...

WHEN TO HOLD ON...

If she's just started bailing on you or acting selfish, she might be stressed, or be having issues at home. Ask if she's okay, and let her know you're there for her, but if it continues, move to the next step.

WHEN TO REPAIR IT...

If she's made you feel bad or mad, when you're alone with her, say 'I feel like you're (insert her action), and that hurts.' She may not realise how nasty she's being and will shape up straight away, if however she doesn't try to change, move to the next step.

HOW TO BREAK IT OFF...

You can't make someone change; don't get into an argument with her or cause a fuss, if she doesn't seem to care, you know she's no friend of yours, and the best thing you can do is to steer clear of her and keep your distance.

GREEN-EYED MONSTER

Are you constantly comparing yourself to your best bud? Do you turn green with envy at girls who always look great? Here's how to handle it...

IF YOUR MATE GETS MORE THAN YOU DO...

Do you spend entire break times listening to your friend telling you about yet another new addition to her jewellery/shoe/dress collection? If the words 'dad bought me a too-cute necklace' sound familiar, it's no wonder you're feeling seriously envious of her.

DEAL WITH IT Bite your tongue. While it might be tempting to call her a spoiled brat, it won't help. Your friend may get lots of lovely gifts and treats but take a look at your own world, okay, so you might not have the latest trainers, but you probably get more of the really important stuff from your folks – like love, time and attention. And don't demand more from your parents.

IF YOUR BEST MATE ALWAYS LOOKS GREAT...

Shopping with your mate is a complete 'mare and something you should try to avoid. While she looks fabulous in everything she tries on, you're having a total 'I-hate-myself-nothing-looks right' moment in the dressing room.

DEAL WITH IT The comparisons stop here, okay? You're not your friend, you're a complete one-of-a-kind version of you, which is a good thing. So instead of turning green at the way your friend is working a particular outfit, work out which colours and styles look good on you and experiment with them.

Sometimes it just takes a few cool accessories to give your confidence a boost. Don't try to be a carbon-copy of your friend, be a super-cool you instead!

IF YOUR SIS GETS AWAY WITH EVERYTHING...

Your younger sister is able to wrap your parents around her little finger and whatever she wants, she instantly gets. This jealousy inducer is a common nark with older sisters, when you feel younger sibs are getting an easier ride, it's very difficult not to turn a deep shade of unflattering green.

Over the last couple of years you've done all the hard work with your parents – arguing over curfews and pocket money and now she's sitting back and enjoying the later curfews and enjoying the benefits. Whether she gets bought more stuff than you or goes to bed later than you did at her age there's simply no point moaning. Instead, start thinking of her as the baby of the family, feel incredibly pleased with yourself that you've done such a good deed and enjoy being the more mature one.

IF YOUR MATE HAS A NEW LAD...

Your best friend is dating her first ever boyfriend and she's ditching your nights out faster than last year's pink sparkly eyeshadow trend. You're jealous of him for getting all her attention and you're stomping your foot about her landing herself a cute lad.

*

Listen, kissing your Mcfly poster goodnight is not the closest you'll ever get to romance, promise! It's a fact that some boys really are quite cute, but they're not essential in order to have a fun-packed, I-love-life vibe. Your dream boy will come along when the time is right. In the mean time, make a few new mates to share girl-time with and don't get angry at your mate or ditch her for bagging a boy, give her time to hang out with her new beau and just tell her gently you never seem to see her any more and that you miss her. This way, you'll know she'll be sticking around when you start dating too.

IF YOUR CRUSH LIKES SOMEONE ELSE...

You have a jumbo-sized crush on the lush lad in your maths class, the trouble is, he doesn't know you exist. In fact, you've even noticed him flirting with another girl and this has got you thinking that there must be something really wrong with you and that she must have something that you haven't, yep, she's flicked your jealousy switch.

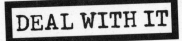 **DEAL WITH IT** Woah, hold up! While it might be really tempting, don't be mean to the other girl. It's not her fault he likes her is it? Chances are, if he doesn't know you exist, it's because you haven't introduced your fabulous self! Be brave and talk to your crush. Show him what a cool, funny and fantastic person you really are. If after hanging out for a while, it's clear that he just wants to be mates, accept it. The boy clearly has no taste and it's now time to find a lad that appreciates how fab and gorgeous you are, okay?!

BEAT THE GREEN-EYED MONSTER

• **Be confident** Look in the mirror and love the girl staring back at you, why would you want to be someone else when you're really rather fabulous just as you are?!

• **Treat yourself** Why wait for a boy to take you to the cinema or to buy you chocolates or flowers? Buy them for yourself! You'll become a self-esteem queen who knows that she deserves the very best.

• **Boost your bravado** Don't be afraid to experiment with different looks and styles, take inspiration from celebs and friends, but don't copy them, be unique!

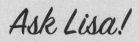

Ask Lisa!

Life coach and *mizz* magazine's Agony Aunt, Lisa Clark answers your friend-related problems.

My mate is so boring! When she comes and calls for me, I say can we do something fun but she never says yes, she just plays on my computer or watches telly. This is making me feel very fed up. What should I do?

I'd suggest a fun day out with your friend. Text her or call her up and ask if she wants to go swimming or to do something you'll both enjoy. If she says no and asks if she can just come round yours just tell her that you're still going. She should respect that you want to do what you want sometimes and if she asks to go on the computer or watch TV, just ask to do something more fun. Don't tell her she's boring but drop a few hints that you'd like to do something else for a change.

There's this girl in my class and, she says I'm her friend – but she talks about me behind my back, pushes me around and calls me names. She's really popular and gets all my friends to fall out with me. What should I do?

This girl is definitely not your friend if she's treating you like this. The best thing to do is ignore her if she calls you names and don't just agree to be friends with her when she says sorry, 'cos you know she'll do it again. If she carries on treating you this way you should tell someone 'cos nobody should have to put up with this behaviour – it's bullying. Try and hang with some different friends as this particular gang is making you unhappy.

Please help, I'm lonely. My two best mates leave me out all the time because they have friends of their own. They are always texting each other and I feel left out. I've tried talking to them but they just act in the same way. I don't have anyone to talk to. What should I do?

If your friends are treating you this way then they're not really acting like your friends. Maybe you could try getting to know their friends better so you can all hang out in a group? If that doesn't work, arrange fun days out with all your friends so you start one big gang. Your friends will love having loads more friends and you'll be happy and popular! You could also join local clubs where you could meet new people. It may be daunting at first but once you get over your initial shyness, it could be a blast!

CHAPTER SIX
MAD ABOUT THE BOY

Sometimes it feels like lads are from a different planet. Check out the mizz crash course in the opposite sex...

FIND OUT IF A BOY FANCIES YOU (WITHOUT LOOKING DESPERATE)

DO	DON'T
♂ Ask your mates to dig around for information for you. Subtly!	♂ Ask his friends what he thinks. They'll just tell him and you'll feel like a fool.
♂ Pay attention. If you catch him looking at you, he's interested.	♂ Stare him out. It's not very cool and you might just scare him off.
♂ Smile when you catch his eye. If he holds eye contact and smiles back, result!	♂ Give up if he doesn't smile back when you smile at him. Lads can be shy too, y'know.
♂ Check his chemistry. If his pupils get bigger and his lips redder when he's speaking to you, he likes you – big time.	♂ Yelling 'cute booty' as he walks past is not attractive. Don't do it!

HOW TO... FLIRT WITHOUT HIM EVEN KNOWING

Before you start, tell yourself this: you're confident and you're interesting. And flirting is fun, not an ancient form of social torture, so enjoy it.

LAUGH

Forget playing with your hair and pouting like a model. That's not flirting, that's an open invite. Okay for some, but the subtle flirt knows lads like girls who are happy and fun to be around.

ACT INTERESTED

Ask him lots of questions — lads love to talk about themselves. Weirdly, after you've focussed on him all night, he'll come away thinking that you're the fascinating one. Boys, huh?!

FLATTER HIS EGO

You don't need to come over all art-girl and gush about the poetry in his soul. A compliment like "Where's your top from? It's really nice," will do.

BOY TALK

So there's this lad you like and you want to talk to him, except you've got butterflies in your belly, your palms are sweaty and your mouth's gone dry, right? Here's how to rock your convo skills so that you can talk to boys in any situation!

Smile!

Before you even open your mouth to speak, your body is making a first impression. So if you're standing with your hands on your hips and pulling a model-girl pout, you're saying to the world 'I've got attitude' without saying a single word. The trick is to make yourself as approachable and fun to be around as possible. If lads feel comfortable around you, it'll make talking to them a whole lot easier.

TALKING TIPS **When you're about to approach a boy, make yourself as open as possible, keep your arms unfolded, and most importantly, smile! If you look like you are approachable and easy to talk to, the boys will come to you!**

Work it out!

What's your conversation goal? It's good to know where you want the convo to go before it starts. Do you want to let him know that you're interested in him? Do you just want to catch up and have a laugh? It's not cool to plan exactly what you're going to say because you don't want to sound like you're reading from a script, but if you know what you want from the conversation, you can make a plan for how you'll achieve it.

TALKING TIPS **One good way to break the ice with a lad, is to be totally honest with him and**

94

tell him what you want. For example, if you're talking to a lad you're crushing on and you really want to know whether he's single or seeing someone, you could say something like, "When I walked over to speak to you, I promised myself I wouldn't leave until I found out if you had a girlfriend or not!" Make sure you say this with a smile and it will sound cute and flattering rather than over-confident and pushy.

Positive visualisation

Before you approach a boy give yourself a pep talk. Our thoughts influence our mood and our behaviour so concentrate on happy thoughts. Dismiss any negative vibes and substitute them with positive ones. If you think that someone is going to laugh in your face or find what you are saying boring, you are likely to feel sad, anxious and defeated and it will come across when you speak.

TALKING TIPS **If you remember all the compliments you have been given or a time when you had a friend in stitches laughing, you are likely to feel happy, calm and confident. Visualise success and it is more likely to occur.**

Be fabulous

Be yourself, not a clone of him. Believe it or not, boys don't want you to be a girl-version of them, that's what their boy mates are for, so don't think you have

to say what you think they want to hear. There's nothing more annoying for a boy than when a girl goes along with everything he says. Don't be afraid to express likes and dislikes or to share opinions. Your tastes and views don't have to be the same as the lad you're talking to. You don't have to listen to the same music, or support the same football team, either. It's really okay to disagree with his opinions as long as you're respectful. Standing up for what you believe in shows you're confident and it also gives him the chance to get to know the real you and what you're passionate about.

TALKING TIPS **If a boy asks what you'd like to eat or what movie you'd like to see, don't say, "I don't mind" or "Whatever you want".** **He'll be asking because he's genuinely interested in what you think or he isn't confident about what to suggest, so if you want to eat Italian and see the new chick flick, give him an honest response.**

Getting what you want

Once you've got the lad you like's attention, there are a few tried and tested tricks for keeping it. The most important thing is to show a genuine interest in him. Smile at him, maintain eye contact, maybe touch his arm to emphasise a point. If you're feeling self-conscious, an added benefit of getting a boy to talk about himself is that it takes the spotlight off you. Once he starts confiding, you'll feel more relaxed and will be able to talk about yourself too.

TALKING TIPS **People love talking about themselves so try asking him questions. Keep it simple, like, what music do you listen to? What's**

it like living at your place? How do you get on with your family? What's the best holiday you've ever been on? What do you like to do on weekends?

Watch and learn

Observe others and then develop your own style. Pay attention to the girls who are more confident and flirty. Not everyone is born with killer convo skills, but anyone can develop them. Mix what works with your own style.

TALKING TIPS Watch confident girls in action and take note of exactly what they say, do, and even what mannerisms they use. Don't copy but learn and develop your own skills. As long as it seems natural there's no harm in getting a little help from others!

WHAT QUESTIONS COULD I ASK A LAD?

Write down some ideas for questions below. This will make you feel more confident when you end up chatting to a boy you like.

. . . .

. . . .

. . . .

. . . .

. . . .

. . . .

IT'S GOOD TO TALK

BELIEVE IN YOURSELF

If other girls have been able to talk to boys, you can too. It's all about having confidence in yourself. If you suspect that others are seeing you in a negative light, your anxiety will get the best of you and you will reflect just that.

LOOK YOUR BEST

You don't have to wear too-tight jeans or too much make-up. Wear clothes you really like and accessorise, so that your ensemble can make your inner beauty stand out. With make-up, remember that 'less is more.' Too much is off-putting, especially when it comes off on your clothes! Keep your hair clean and out of your face so the boy you're talking to you can see your eyes.

★
Step
3

INTRODUCE YOURSELF

Sometimes boys can be shy too and don't have the courage to come up to a girl and say hello. You can introduce yourself with a simple "hello" and a nice, sincere compliment. Chances are that he will appreciate the compliment and want to tell you all about himself. Think – nothing ventured, nothing gained. If you discover that he has a girlfriend, laugh. Don't feel embarrassed. So what? He'll be flattered.

Read his body language

IF HE...	IT MEANS...
Touches his mouth	He's lying
Looks away/rubs his eyes	He's avoiding something
Touches his ear	He's getting impatient
Scratches his neck	He's unsure or insecure
Crosses his arms	He's shy or tense
Sits holding an ankle	He's stubborn
Tilts his head	He's interested
Drops his chin down	He's judging you
Tucks his thumbs into his belt/jeans	He fancies you
Turns his shoulders/ feet towards you	He definitely fancies you

HOW TO SAY "HMMM, YOU'RE CUTE!" IN THREE LANGUAGES

"OHHH, TU ES MIGNON."
FRENCH

"AYYYY, ESTAS GUAPO."
SPANISH

"EHH, SEI CARINO."
ITALIAN

You know you're dating when...

 You've been together more than three weeks.

 You've got a regular, fulfilling text life – in fact, he sends you texts before you do!

 You're automatically invited to his mates' parties.

 He's come round to meet your parents – and even changed his tee for the occasion.

 You can call him whenever you feel like it without worrying that you're needy or sad.

 He tells everyone you're his girlfriend – ahhh.

GETTING OVER HIM

When true love turns into game over, follow our guide to dealing with the downer of getting dumped.

STAGE 1 : INDULGE

Wallow for at least three days. Refuse phone calls (but check your phone every five minutes) and cry a complete river as you look through old photos of you both together.

STAGE 2 : GIRL TIME

Spend time with your mates talking about all the bad things about him, it's time to wash that boy right outta your hair with a gal-pal makeover. If you can't afford a new haircut or a new lipstick, ask your friends to bring round copies of mizz and their make-up bags to re-create a new look.

STAGE 3 : GET OUT THERE

Make plans for future fun. Flirt with your boy mates
to remind yourself why they love you. Accept
every invite whether it's to a party or a night at the
bowling alley. Act like you're in love with life and
pretty soon, you actually will be.

REMEMBER, NO MATTER HOW 'RIGHT' HE SEEMED, IF HE DIDN'T WANT A KICK-ASS GIRL LIKE YOU, HE WAS OBVIOUSLY TOTALLY 'WRONG'.

BOYS: BUSTED!

Your 5 ultimate boy behaviour questions answered.

➜ *Why does he never reply to my texts and how many kisses should I use?*

Whether he's just playing it cool or has a valid excuse for not getting back to you, bombarding him with messages won't make him text back any quicker. It may even have the opposite effect. Relax, be patient and think logically. Perhaps he's in a lesson, at the footie or with his mates. Lads don't text girls when they're hanging with their crew – it's just not the done thing. And if he never replies? Then he's obviously a loser, so don't waste anymore text time on him. If you feel like putting a kiss, do so but stop over-thinking it. If he texts back with a kiss he likes you, if he doesn't he may not be interested. Leave it there and move on.

➜ *Why can't lads talk about their feelings?*

Lads are rarely encouraged to open up and would rather talk about anything else but their emotions. Girls discuss personal stuff from a young age but to boys, intimate can often mean embarrassing. So give them time to get used to the idea and bear in mind that, once they start spilling, they might not stop!

→ Why do boys have to be so competitive and show off all the time?

Girls are always telling each other how great they look, how well they're dressed and how clever they are. Boys don't get this kind of direct approval from their mates. So they need to make sure they're the ones who get it from their girlfriends by 'proving their worth' at every available opportunity.

→ Why can boys never admit they're in the wrong?

They're scared of being shown up by girls. So, if it comes to the crunch, they'll often go so far as to convince themselves that they're right. The test here is the sincerity of a boy's apology if he does say sorry! This will tell you whether you should hitch him or ditch him.

→ Why do boys never want to commit?

There's a whole, big world out there waiting to be discovered. Just 'cause he won't commit, it doesn't mean that he's not into you. It's just that, for him, there's a lot more to see and do. This should be the same for you too. You're only in your teens, so what's the rush? Take it slow and focus on having fun while you can!

Write your love notes here